WELCOME
TO MY
WORLD

*Reflections on
Growing Old Gracefully*

*by
Albert Lyon*

Pittsburgh, PA

SterlingHouse Publisher

ISBN 1-56315-256-8

Poetry
© Copyright 2000 Albert Lyon
All rights reserved
First Printing—2000
Library of Congress #99-65308

Request for information should be addressed to:

SterlingHouse Publisher, Inc.
The Sterling Building
440 Friday Road
Pittsburgh, PA 15209
www.sterlinghousepublisher.com

Cover Design: Michelle S. Vennare—SterlingHouse Publisher, Inc.
Typesetting: Teresa M. Parkman

Printed in Canada

Dedication

To my wife Virginia who was by my side for over
thirty-three years. She was my inspiration and the
one I wrote all my poetry for. I miss her so much and
it is so hard to work without her presence.
When I wrote something, I would read it to her.
I could always tell if it was good, bad, or somewhere
in between by the way it was received.
Many of my works hit the wastebasket
without revision because of her accute sense
of literary value.

I think she always knew that she would not live to
see my work published. She was right.
She slipped away to be with her Lord and
Savior on May 9th 1998. It is hard for me now to
carry on without her and her fabulous contribution to
my life. I dedicate this to my beloved Virginia
Mae Wallace Lyon My Queen.

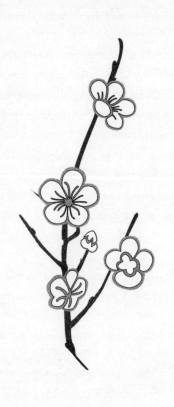

Table of Contents

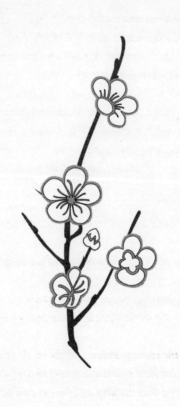

I Had No Idea

I had no idea what this Lady meant to me
I knew I loved her dearly, as any fool could see
I honored her and cherished her and spoiled her all I could
I told her that I loved her less often than I should.

I had no idea of the wonderful surprise
As I met his comely redhead and looked deep into her eyes
I stretched my hand out slowly as if I was in a trance
I stammered rather weakly, "Would the Lady care
to dance?"

She took my hand and smiled and curtsied, and we glided
on the floor
To the strains of Big band melodies we'll remember
evermore.
She was just as beautiful as those on movie screens
She glided on the dance floor with the bearing of a Queen.

By the time the evening ended and the music ceased to play
I knew that I'd been smitten in a very special way.
I took her home that evening and we sat and talked,
til dawn
I asked to see her once again. "I'll call you when I'm gone."

I returned days later and I asked her for a date
I knew she was a treasure and I didn't hesitate
I told her that I loved her and I want her for my wife
She said, "I'll be your woman for the balance of my life."

She slipped away to be with Jesus a little while ago
She was ill and she was tired, she knew it was time to go
I had no idea how painful loneliness could seem
'Til I reached the end of all those years of living
with a Queen

I had no idea why my God had chosen me
To be the honored lover of an Angel such as she
To be graced with all the love and wisdom she possessed
Was like being the custodian of God's own treasure chest.

I had no idea when we danced that hardwood floor
It would generate a love affair which would last
forever more
I had no idea nor could I have ere forseen
How very lonely I will be 'til I am with my Queen.

The Old Wagon Wheel

Just an old wagon wheel on a stake in the barn
all covered with cobwebs and dust.
One broken spoke and a loose iron tire
that was pitted and covered with rust.

You can see, if you try, the old weld in the steel
that joins the beginning and end.
It put me in mind of our great loving God
and His business conducted with men.

Our Bible, God's word, is so much like that wheel
In the beginning it says in the Word.
A man was placed in a garden of love
to tend it and worship the Lord.

He was given a woman and given a work
and given a choice of his own.
So sin he did choose and the garden did lose
and the wheel was beginning to turn.

Not many years more and the world was corrupt
God looked and His great heart was broke.
For the sin of the world came wafting on high
like a billowing cloud of black smoke.

So God did decide to drown in a tide
the filth which had covered the earth.
He raised up a man who was righteous
to give mankind a new birth.

The wheel was now rolling, it came to full circle,
The flood was a definite end.
But notice how close is a brand new start
and the wheel will turn over again.

Beginnings it seems with its high, lofty dreams
is pure in the heart of God's men.
But purity fades and ideals are tainted
And the old wheel is turning again.

In Ur of Chaldees God had chosen a man
to be the father of nations.
He was told of God whereever he trod
would be his for all of creation.

Now some years later, after many mistakes
after many transgressions of sin
The family of kindred descended from him
Were held bondage by evil mean men.

Moses, I'm told, shunned all Egypt's gold
and lead the Children of God to be free.
King David's stout hand gave them Caanan
then what happened next still puzzles me.

And so down the road one more episode
Of God's love and the failure of men
The end of one story, another beginning
and the old wheel is turning again.

Now a brand new beginning, He was born in a manger
At a time of subjection in old Bethlehem.
And so it was told by the prophets of old
He is King of creation, Son of Mighty, "I Am."

The wheel was now turning, His life was unfolding
Righteousness and mercy prevailed in His hand.
Soon He would suffer and die on a cross
And His blood would spill over to save sinful man.

Oh, the terrible sorrow and feeling of loss
was short as they laid Him away in a cave.
On the first lovely morning according to scripture
He is risen, resurrection has come from the grave.

The Glory of God sprang forth from the sod.
The Angels told Mary and Mary told men
Now forever God's proven His love for us all
And the old wheel turned over again.

My Flag

I strained my eyes to see it as it fluttered in the breeze
Down the shade-lined street with its tall green stately trees
There was stirring martial music and the drum of
marching feet
Then my heart just leaped inside me, as I prepared to greet

MY FLAG

It was not the music, the oration, or the band
It was not the muffled drums that cause our
Nation's stand
The patriotic feeling as I watch "Old Glory" wave
The chills that travels up my spine I'll carry to my grave

I LOVE MY FLAG

It floated over Valley Forge, bloody footprints in the snow
Over countless daily sacrifice of some we'll never know
She has writhed in holy anguish through the early
growing pains.
She has seen our country patiently through sunny
days and rains

Don't you know of what I'm speaking, can't you feel t
he awsome pride
The feeling of belonging that wells up from deep inside
When you hear your nation's anthem, see her gently
waving high
Just to think of all she means to me, it makes me
want to cry
I'm a sentimentalist, pardon if I brag
We're speaking of the land I love

WE'RE TALKING 'BOUT MY FLAG

The Music Box

I owned a precious music box when I was just a boy
Some folks thought it trivial, 'twas just a small child's toy
It was more than that you see, it meant the world
and all to me.
And, oh the joyful, cheerful glee, as I heard the music
made for me

Inside the lid the face of Christ would look at me with
eyes so kind
Then the music would swell up and fill my heart and
soul and mind
I didn't know the words back then, I only knew the tune.
As I watched the face of Jesus glow, the music filled
the room
It quieted all my fears, you see, because the song was j
ust for me.

*Many years have come and gone since the music box
was mine*
*I know not when it left my care, what happened or
what time*
*I was grown into a man and memories fade and die
each day*
I hadn't really realized how far my childhood slipped away
*I forgot the face of Jesus Christ and what His song had
meant to me*

*And then one day the whole of God and Jesus' glowing
smiling face*
*Came crashing into focus as I heard men sing
"Amazing Grace"*
*"Amazing Grace, how sweet the sound that saved a
wretch like me"*
*Was the words that matched the music that's been
gone so long from*

ME

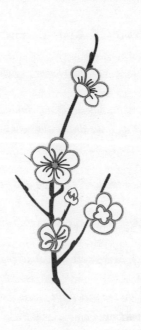

The Hill

I had a dream the other night when everything was still
In this dream I started climbing up a high steep endless hill
I stopped in many lovely spots to rest along the way
I looked at things around me that beckoned me to stay

But something deep inside me seemed to urge me to the top
And though I'm tired and weary now I know I dare
not stop
I was young when this dream started now age has
come on me
But the climbing still continues and I'm weary now you see

Through a thick and dark cloud layer I struggle ever higher
And now I see the pinnacle, this is my soul's desire
And now I see a level spot to pause for final rest.
I sat down and looked around me, I had made it
to the crest

A man stood there beside me and stretched out a
wounded hand
He said, "Now that you are up here, Son, I know y
ou'll understand
I was the voice which prodded you each time you
paused to rest
I was the strength you needed not to stop at
second best
I brought you through the darkened cloud to
the level top, you see
Because I planned that you would spend eternity
with Me."

Grandpa, What's It Feel Like Growing Old?

My eyes were just about half closed,
I'd started dozing in my chair
My grandson's voice came loud and clear
and filled the room from everywhere

His eyes were bright portraying youth with
ever-present honesty
A mind that reaches out for bits to ease his curiosity
This boy has asked some questions that it would
take a sage
To conjure up the answers he demanded for his age.

So when he asked me, "Grandpa, what's it feel like
growing old?"
I had to study long and hard for answers to be told
"In the first place my, dear grandson, I don't feel I've
grown old yet!
I'm on my way and this I'll say 'til now I've scant regret.

I've gained a bit of knowledge and some scars
along the way
I have more aches and pains today than I had yesterday
I think what you are asking, what you'd really
like to know
If I could do it over would I really care to go.

Would I trade, if God allowed it, a few of my todays
To relive a year or maybe more of younger yesterdays
No, son, my days are precious, each a jewel in purest gold.
And I think this is the greatest of rewards for growing old

My days are filled with loving friends, my nights are
filled with dreams
My years are filled with memories-life's bursting at
the seams
Now life is one great trade-off and in my older age
I've gained.
Oh, the things like youth and stamina and exuberance
has waned
They've given way to wisdom expectation, peace of soul
A grace that passes understanding now that Christ
is in control."

The Angel
With Her Magic Pots And Pans

My mother was a genius with food and pots and pans
How she managed still gives me pause to smile.
With a minimum of meager food components
She could make an inch of meat look like a mile.

As long as she had eggs and lard and flour
A little salt and onion by her side
Some coffee and a stockpot and some flavors
We always left the table satisfied.

Her heart was always into simple fixings
So her family always had some wholesome food.
She never failed to make a little sweetness
A pie, a cake, or pudding for her brood.

When I think about the feeding of five thousand
I see a specter of my mother standing there
An angel in an apron, with a skillet in her hand.
Poised before an open, empty Frigidaire.

I remember tomato soup made out of ketchup
And a brown flour water gravy she could make.
Several dozen high-rising soda biscuits
As light and full of flavor as a cake.

She turned sugar and maple flavor into candy
And miracles were wrought before our eyes
With love and care and patience she would labor
To produce a tasty succulent surprise.

If my Daddy was the strength to guide the family
With the fate of our survival in his hands
Mama was the glue which held it all together
The angel with her magic pots and pans.

Daddy Was A Giant Of A Man

My dad stood six foot one inch tall
With curly hair and dark brown eyes
He weighed about two hundred pounds
And looked slender for his size
His hair grayed early in his teens
The same as mine, to no surprise.

Long before us kids were born
He served his flag in France
He was always first to volunteer
He was always first to take a chance
He could be counted to take a noble stand
He was always first to step in line
My Daddy was a giant of a man

You couldn't really measure
By the money that he made
The way the world measures out success
He did it all without complaining
And the total price was paid
He never settled short, for nothing less
His friends could always trust him
Like a dollar in their hand
My daddy was a giant of a man

Sometimes Dad went hungry
So us kids could have the food
Each Christmas there were presents and a tree
It was during this awful crucial time
When job work wasn't good
How he pulled it all together puzzles me
With the worry and the pain, I will say again
MY Daddy was a giant of a man.

Just A Little Tag-a-Long

My brother was the first born; he was handsome,
tall, and strong
He was always Momma's favorite, and I knew
that all along
Then came little sister, so demure, so sweet, and shy
She was the plum of Daddy's orchard, the apple
of his eye.

When I was born it seemed to me there's nowhere I belong
I was last and least, an afterthought. Just a little
Tag-a-long
When we chose up sides for baseball games, if I got
chose at all
It wasn't 'cause I was wanted but the fact I owned
the ball

It seemed a life of hand-me-downs, and games of
odd man out
I stood beside the road of life with an overwhelming doubt
Til now I've never had a break, no one ever sang my song
And I had the feeling for all my life, I'm a useless
Tag-a-long

One night at a revival, at the invitation song
People headed for the altar, so I thought I'd tag along
Preacher prayed with all who came; as usual I was last.
All others cried and prayed a lot. He turned to me
and asked:

"Will you give your heart to Jesus, to the Savior
you'll belong
And you'll shed that worldly image of a little tag-a-long."
Then I heard the Master speak to me, "Come to Me
and take your rest
You'll be dining at My mansion, you will be My
honored guest
You are loved and you are sanctified as a member
of My throng.
Now remember you're no longer just a little Tag-A-Long."

You Can't Get There From Here

I was driving through the Ozarks on a gorgeous
scenic route
I stopped at a rustic roadside store and decided to find out
If I could get to Washita by staying on this route.
The map was so confusing with the lakes and hills and all
I asked the old attendant just to see could he recall
If I stay upon this crooked road that wound through
Arkansas
Would I come upon the little town that's known as
Washita?

"Let me see," the old man pondered as he sipped upon
his beer
His finger traced around the map, "You can't get there
from here!"
"You should have turned at Blue Springs town to take
two ninety eight
and now you're near to Hollis Town; go back 'fore it's
too late."
I didn't want to turn around, let's find another way
Look here, this seems to be a route that's bound to save
the day.
Let's take this route called three-fourteen, then left at
twenty-seven
It's crooked mountain highway, it'll be more hell
than heaven

We traveled west on three-fourteen, this way there
was no doubt.
In forty miles a barrier-the bridge had been washed out.
A hopeless feeling struck me and it filled my heart with
fear
As I recalled the old man's words, "You can't get there
from here!"
It reminds me of the struggle and what some folks have
to pay
When they try to find salvation and they do it their
own way
There's one door to the Kingdom, and Jesus has the key
When He said He was the only way, that's good enough
for me
Don't try to work salvation out yourself, let's make
this clear
As the old man told me long ago, "You can't get there
from here!"

The Cash Register

It was new and it was shiny, made of glass and brass
and steel
It had a marble change plate that was like velvet to
the feel
A big brass handle on its side, keys protruded from
its face
It stood nearly two foot tall upon its counter space.

When the money was collected, tabulator keys would bring
The sum to appear behind the glass, and a little bell
would ring
The slot machine-type handle, pulled down with certain
flair
The drawer popped open down below, the cash was
placed in there.

It was a trusted proud machine, the owner's pride was
in the thing.
Then one day to all's dismay the bell refused to ring.
They called up a mechanic to restore the tinkling sound.
Alas, there's nothing he could do to make the bell resound.

They sold the once proud register to a dealer secondhand
For a register without a bell was not much in demand
It was still bright and shiny, all parts still working right
But without a bell it wouldn't sell if you tried with all
your might.

A man came in the store one day, and pulled the
handle down
The bottom drawer flew open and the bell refused to sound.
He said to the proprietor, "I'll take this one today
I'll give you what you're asking if you'll deliver
right away."

The proprietor, dumbfounded, took the customer aside
He said, "This is a fine machine, but one thing I must
not hide
All parts are working smartly, but I warn you of one thing
When you tally up a sale on this the bell will never ring."

The customer began to smile, his face was all aglow
I'm so glad you told me, but my son will never know
Because it's bright and shiny and it works real good,
you see
Is all that really matters, because he's also deaf like me."

100 Pounds Of Steel

Would you give me several minutes of your ever
precious time
There's a lesson to be learned in this story set to rhyme.
I'll tell you of four gentlemen, and I think you'll get
the feel
Of what each man could accomplish with one hundred
pounds of steel.

The first man we must call the fool, for his shortness
of sight
His lack of imagination, ambition, guts, and fight
He sold the hundred pounds of steel for scrap so he
could eat
He traded off a legacy for a bite of daily meat.

The second more successful man took the hundred
pounds of steel
And worked with ingenuity-opportunities were real.
He multiplied investment to ten times the normal sales
He hammered the hundred pounds of steel into a hundred
pounds of nails

The third man wasn't satisfied with a mere tenfold
in gain
He studied market strategy and he pushed his fertile
brain
What can I make that people want, what is in great
demand?
What will get a hundred fold with the steel that's in
my hand?
With a stroke of utter genius he filled some empty bins
With thousands upon thousands of forever useful pins.

The fourth is last but never least, he must be set apart.
Some say that he is lucky, others say that he is smart.
With the hundred pounds of steel he built a whole
new industry
His name was Adolph Gruen and he built a watch
for me.

Heros

When I was just a boy I held my dad in awe
And I had a lot of heroes to admire.
A lot of folks who gave me pride to imitate
To a boy it was my heart's desire.
To hit a clutch home run in the bottom of the ninth
Or to run like Jesse Owens who set the pace.
Just pretend that I'm the hero who invented
The vaccine we need to save the human race.

There were cowboys who rode the silver screen
Who wore white hats and fought with evil men
They never killed a bad man outright.
They brought them back to justice way back then.

Who can our kids look up to and emulate today?
A Clint Eastwood, J.R. Ewing, or Stallone
People of deceit and violence replete.
With language that's unfit to grace our home.

Where have all the heroes gone from yesteryear?
Red Grange, and Bobby Feller, and Tom Mix.
Men of strong, impeccable conviction
Who could win without a bunch of dirty tricks.

It's a shame our fine young football players
Pump their bodies full of steroids for an edge.
Young athletic hopefuls taking LSD and coke.
Have battered mind and body like a sledge.

Our value system's taken quite a beating
Situation ethics reign from dark to dawn
Now I ask the question and repeat it once again
Where in the world have all our heroes gone?

If our kids have no one left to look up to
They will fall into Satan's pit that's just beyond
It won't matter in the future the question I had asked
Where in God's name have all our heroes gone?

The Ballad of a Strange, Strange Boy

He was a strange boy, lived high up in them hills
Only meat he ever eat was what his pappy kills
He had no truck with other kids, he never had
no money
Never had a store bought haircut and dressed so
dadburn funny.

He never talked until he thought, as though he had
no sense
He dreamed and lived within himself, why folks
thought he was dense
He writ down every thing he heard, an' read a lot at night.
He had to fill that head of his, he didn't seem too bright.

I remember back in '24 he took a schoolin' test,
I understand in all land he scored up as the best.
They sent him off to doctor's school, and even
paid his way.
In seven years he came back home to doctor and to stay.

Then came the flu in '32 and lots of folks took sick.
The wintertime was long and hard and hit with
quite a kick
The snow piled high to block the roads, so nothing
could come in,
No food, no clothes, no dry goods stores, no precious
medicine.

On snowshoes made of barrel staves, he wrestled with
high snow.
To treat sick, dying neighbors while supplies were
getting low.
He prayed beside the sick ones when the medicine ran out.
I knew God heard and lent a hand, of this I had no doubt.

The sickness ran its evil course, the doctor's health
was broke
He had given all he had back then, and died of
massive stroke
Some died that year, but most survived, remember
if you can
You live today 'cause a strange, strange boy became
a godly man.

The Stranger With A Cane

Out of nowhere one day came a well dressed man
Who had a limp and carried a cane
He walked into hall where the town came to meet
We assume he'd arrived on the train
He was dress for the evening in black tie and cloak
With a top hat and ebony cane
His demeanor commanded the awe of us all
Who met there at Center and Main.

He presented a contrast to all the townfolk
Who were met to consider our plight.
Our factory had moved, we were all out of work
Our future was black as the night.
In the midst of this panic solutions were nil
The stranger stepped up to the table
"Let me lighten your burden, if that be your will
I'll assist you as much as I'm able."

I have money you need to buy your spring seed
You can pay back the loan with your crop
And here is a loan to keep you in food
'Til you're productive and back on the top".
"Dear benevolent friend, you have given us hope
You're so good, so kind, and so nice
We accept 'cause we know you love deeply
And we'er not even asking the price".

In those hours of blind desperation
We were eagerly groping at straws
We sold out to a quick fix from Satan
Now we're caught in the serpent's strong jaws.
We can't pay the money advanced that we owe
The stranger is now in control
He'll lend us a little more now and again,
And the price he will ask is our soul.

I glanced at the cane standing close by his desk
I saw the large carved silver head.
It was that of a hideous serpent
Evil features and horrers to dread

Why didn't I go to the Father in prayer
When hopeless entered my life
instead of solutions the world seems to offer
To tempt me in trouble and strife
Is it too late for me now to ask Jesus
In prayer to break Satan's control
After God defeated him there at the cross
To purchase the deed to our soul

The Gathering Storm

Dark clouds hide the mountains
And you know there'll be a storm
The wind is blowing stronger
And it isn't near as warm
We can see the signs of weather
And we're blind to signs of time
And we'er stumbling down the highways
Paying no heed to the signs.

Now Jesus told us plainly
We know how to read the sky
But we cannot see the danger
'Til it takes us by and by
There's corruption in high places
And our love is growing cold

There is many wars and pestilance
and the evil one grows bold.
Is it time, oh Lord, to meet us
In the sky as you have said
To raise those souls who died in Christ
As though they were not dead
Yet I know that you will tarry
Though the time be so depraved
'Til the saints of God have harvested
All the souls tha You want saved

Oh Watchman

It's funny how we never miss a person 'til he's gone
We expect that he will be there every day
We take our friends for granted, in moments they are gone
And in passing we do not know what to say

I should have told that person that I loved him
But you see, I didn't take the time
I got so used to having him around me
I didn't think we'd e'er run out of time

Then one day he slipped away forever
His passing left a lonely broken heart
When I think of all the things I could have told him
The hurting makes the teardrops want to start

Many times I tried to tell my friend of Jesus
The thought that I could wait another day
I knew that I could tell him any moment
I had all the answers, all the things to say

Now I know I should have acted quickly
Salvation is too precious not to share
Since my friend had never known of Jesus
His passing is a grief I can not bear.

If you love a person tell him of the savior
Oh Watchman you're the keeper of the wall
If you don't sound out the trumpet of salvation
You have never loved that person after all

Time

Time is what God gave to humans
It will be here 'til time is no more
It was given to Adam, the father of man
It will cease the moment we walk through the door.

We won't need it there in the Kingdom
It was meant to be spent here on earth
To be cherished or wasted, remembered or hasted
It started the moment of birth.

When rebellion came strong in man's spirit
His souls seperated in sin
God could not grant him eternity living
So time was then metered to him

Time is man's ponderous restrictions
You only have so much to spend
The time that you wasted is gone forever
The last moment you spent has come to an end.

You can't stop the clock that God started
The moment you took your first breath
It parades without mercy through all of your life
'Til your candle's extinguished in death

I guess the great question to answer
Do you waste time in fancy and whim?
Do you waste time on worldly dimension?
Do you spend it to glorify Him?

Whatever it takes, my dear brother
To know Jesus while I'm in my prime
Will be worth all the gold and the jewels of the world
When I've completely run out of my time.

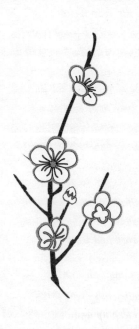

All We Like Sheep

Once I was incensed by the reference to sheep
Which was made in the scriptures of old
How men are compared to those ignorant creatures
Which need to be kept in a fold
By a masterful shepherd who sees to the needs
Of those dumb things that's under his care
I thought I was smarter and stronger by far
To be thought of like that was unfair.

Then I stopped to think of how cruel is the world
When we wander outside of the fold
So the jackals of Satan and the serpents of sin,
Can wound us in body and snipe at our soul
And the foolish each day who go wandering away
Not heeding the Shepherd's great care.
So the wolves can creep up and destroy whom they may
And feast on the foolish out there.

Then I think of the strength in the midst of the flock
And the helpless new lambs that are born
The nurture they get from the milk of the word
'Til they're grown and are fit to be shorn
The temptation is great and the danger is real
Outside of the shepherd's protection
Satan's out there to kill and to steal
No matter the compass direction.

So you see, like the sheep, man is not safe alone
His strength is no match for the world
His intellect no match for Satan
And temptations that's sure to be hurled.
He is helpless outside of the sheep fold
So it doesn't irk me anymore.

A Name Or A Number

God's Kingdom is made up of millions of saints
Who are named in the Lamb's Book of Life
Who are held and protected by God's loving hand
From the soon coming trouble and strife.

God names all His saved, that is told in the word
In a book that's called God's revelation
For each soul is sealed by the blood of our Lord
from unspeakable dark devastation.

For a trumpet will sound and the Church will be called
To meet Jesus high in the air
The graves will then open and saved sleeping saints
Will join us and sup with us there.

How different the fate of the millions of souls
Who are left when the Antichrist reigns
So in order to barter, to buy or to sell
They'll surrender their hearts and their brains.

They'll receive on their forehead the number of man
And be forced by the terrible beast
To worship the counterfeit god of this world
whom Satan has raised from the East.

Having told you what God has declared in the book
And knowing you're called on to choose
How will you decide where your soul will abide
My friend will you win, will you lose?

Will your name be recorded in the Lamb's Book of Life
Or beguiled by the world's dirty tricks?
Will you choose to be sealed by the blood and the cross
Or display the dread six-sixty-six?

When the last curtain falls on the ages
And the last drop is drained from the cup
Will God call your name up in Glory
Or will Satan turn your number up?

The Search

I guess I spent so much time in my searching
I hungered for something I didn't know what.
Down deep inside me a lonliness building
A sweet peace of mind I had all but forgot.

Try as I might to get shed of that feeling
To drown it in liquor or work it to death
Or read and discuss on high lofty subjects
Or pursue worldly wisdom till there's nothing left

Maybe if I had a house in the country
Or if I could travel 'til I had my fill
Or If I had a boat to go fishing on Sunday
That would be something that may fit the bill.

Then I buried my face in sheer desperation
And I cried "Oh Lord God, if you're really alive
You'll give me an answer to this futile existance
I shall go all to pieces and never survive."

Then a voice deep inside me spoke peace to my soul
And a road opened under my feet
Then the word came so plain from the Spirit of God
Now my child after me you repeat:

"Forgive me, dear Jesus, for sin in my life
Come into my heart Holy One
And give me sweet peace that I never could find
And your blessing, Lord let it be done.

"What you ask me to do in the form of a prayer
from the heart of a desperate soul
Was what I had waited so long to hear
For you to give up your control

"That's all that I ask of a sin-blackened soul
Is to turn yourself over to Me
I will blot out your past, make you whiter than wool
A forever sweet savor to Me."

I'll Change,
Lord, I'll Change

My head settled deep in my pillow
And the world slipped slowly away
And sleep ended all of my daily pursuits
And I didn't take much time to pray

My dream started all of a sudden
the dream was all about me
Suddenly with no prior warning
How in the world could it be?

I had died, and it seemed so real
Like a vapor I am floating through space
Now I reach a bright far destination
and behold Jesus' bright smiling face.

He took hold of my hand and He lead me
To where I'll eternally live.
He showed me a small one-room shanty
He said, "This is all I can give."

I said, "I expected a mansion
Isn't that what you said in your word?
Why is my reward quite so meager?
Just one tiny room is absurd."

"My son, I wanted to bless you
With contentment and mansion and crown
but you opted for worldly possessions
For worldly aclaim and renown".

"Remember the word also told you
From the time of your spiritual birth
To lay up your treasures in heaven
Not on this corruptable earth".

"I gave you the substance to serve Me
Each time that you ask in My name
I equipped you to carry salvation
Then I prayed and I waited in vain."

"See that mansion high on the hill top
I reserved that for you just in case.
You would wake in your spirit and serve me,
with faith 'till you finish your race."

I woke, cold sweat on my forehead
As the truth of the dream came to me
It was fraught with my lack of worship
Shortcomings as plain as could be.

I know now the time for my witness
Is now while I'm still in control
and laying up treasures in heaven
a benefit felt deep in my soul

When the Lord tells me, "Son let Me bless you."
I will say, "Lord Christ, here am I."
I will follow His lead in thought and in deed
For the mansion He built in the sky.

Marriage Made In Heaven By Mistake

Come, tell me all the troubles that distress you.
Conditions that cause your heart to ache
You're dissolving your family and your marraige
As a marriage made in heaven by mistake.

You tell me that you just no longer love her
Oh, yes, you loved her truly when you wed
In a few short years affection for her vanished
Now all feeling toward your wife is dead

Of course, the fault's all hers that your marriage
went to bits
You have stood for all the hurt that you can take
And you want to break your vow 'cause you
realize it now
As a marriage made in heaven by mistake

Let me tell you, son, I don't buy that tale of yours
Were you prepared back then to love her all the way.
Then tell me if you can why you cease to love her now
Has she changed all that much since yesterday

Could it be that you were searching an escape hatch
In case fleeting infatuation didn't last?
In your haste to enjoy the sensual pleasures
You ignored the crucial questions that were asked

Did you love her, yes I mean really love her
Were you willing to fulfill her every need
To sacrifice yourself to make her happy
To be unselfish in every thought and deed

When you treat your married life like God commanded
Your wife's response is love, for Jesus' sake
Because a marriage made in heaven under God's
directing hand
Ain't a Marriage Made in Heaven by Mistake.

Garage Sale

I watched a man who nailed a sign
Upon the fence outside
An arrow pointed to the rear
The garage door's open wide.

"Garage sale" scribbled on the sign
I sensed a melancholy air
This cluttered place and the old man's face
As he beckoned from his chair.

Come in, my friend, and look around
And tell me what you see
Some scattered trash, discarded junk
Sentimental potpourri.

There's treasure here that represent
Some fading memory
There's pride, and love, and heartbreak
And a great deal more, you see

You see that rusty sled up there
I bought that for my son
He's gone and I've not seen him now
Since he turned twenty-one.

I'd save it for a grandchild
But, you see, I'll never have one
My children never married
And there'll never be a grandson

Oh, that old rag doll is special
My daughter loved it so
We gave it on her birthday
A long ,long time ago

And then we bought a puppy dog
He was mongrel through and through
And Shep the dog and the old rag doll
Had quite a hoop-de-doo

Shep shook the doll till the eye fell out
Then he bit off dolly's nose
That's my daughter's tears you see
That soiled poor dolly's clothes.

Why Shep! He lived for fourteen years.
He's buried in the yard.
His chain and collar's yonder
My daughter took it hard.

That faded apron hanging yonder
Belonged to my late wife.
I bought it on our honeymoon
And she kept all her life

Of all the things I've given her
There's nothing I recall
That she cherished more'n
That faded apron hanging on the wall

So you see, my friend, I'm all alone
I just don't need these things
To dredge up all the memories
That all this treasure brings.

The kids are grown and fled the nest
My precious wife's with God
And Shep's out there in my backyard,
Resting in the sod.

And I have pleasant dreams at night
So mister take it all
Just leave that faded apron
Where it hangs upon the wall.

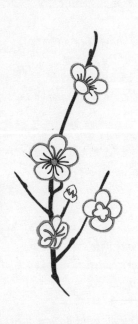